The Cater Waiter's Bride Guide

How to have an elegant and stress-free
wedding without being mocked
by the wait staff.

By Ross Cascio

Cover Art by Jon Sloan

Dedications:

To all my fellow wait staff, banquet servers, captains, supervisors, managers, sales personnel, chefs, cooks, housemen, and dishwashers who provide memories at events throughout the world. Specifically the D'Amico Catering staff at The Metropolitan Ballroom.

To the administrative staff at my full-time job for proofing and editing my story.

The best way for a stress free wedding

is to know things WILL go wrong. As long as you both say "I do," and your priest, minister, rabbi, judge, justice of the peace, or friend who signed up on an on-line officiate website announces, "Husband and Wife," your wedding is a success. You got the job done. If the walls crumble and all your flowers wilt, you'll still be at the end goal, but here are some items and tips to make your day wonderful. What credentials do I have? I work as a banquet server and captain (supervisor) at a company voted as Minneapolis/St. Paul's best catering company for large weddings by <u>Minnesota Bride</u> for four straight years. I was a columnist writing an article on catering in a cake decorating magazine for two years. I've been a best man, an usher, and a lector three times each, a wedding consultant, decorated a reception semi-single handedly (the mother of the bride tried to help, bless her heart), and a personal attendant. Although I've never been a bride, I can empathize.

I'm assuming you got the ring and the date and, therefore, a fiancé. So you've done the hardest part. Have you set the day with ample time to do the entire final planning -- each and every miniscule detail? It depends how quick you can make decisions and stick with them, or if you can't do that, do you trust someone to make those choices for you? If you intend to get your fiancé's opinion – don't bother. He is unlikely to truly care, and in the extreme circumstance he does have an idea – get it early and consciously try to include his thoughts. I wouldn't fret for any zany screwball ideas. He should know what you're good with and comfortable doing. If he seriously thinks you're serving buffalo wings and beer nuts, you may want to rethink the marriage, but we'll discuss themes later. Let's talk about prep work.

PREP WORK

Chances are you've had wedding ideas since you were six, but as you matured, alterations have been made or sacrificed to reality - - no more rainbow unicorns as flower bearers or Cinderella's castle to hold the reception (but I bet you could reserve it through Disney).

First, you know if you're going religious, and therefore, your church. Generally, the bride's church hosts the wedding ceremony. This may mandate your timeline. Some large congregations may be booked years in advance. If you intend to use a cathedral you will need more time and monetary means.

Secular locations, such as a park, may also need time to book. In some instances, your reception can be at the same location, which I've experienced first-hand; but then your party has no "get away" from guests time, as you move right from "I do" to "I eat." On the plus side, you'll never lose a guest or crazy Aunt Sarah en route to the reception. Of course, there is the justice of the peace, and if you're considering that, skip to the chapter on reception.

COLORS

I believe the color for your wedding is twofold:

> Complimentary to the season
> Complimentary to bride

You don't want peach in an autumn wedding any more than you want burnt umber in summer. Avoid "holiday" color schemes. Red and green at Christmas will only SCREAM CHRISTMAS, and red and blue will be too patriotic, unless you're marrying a Senator.

Here are some suggestions for the main color:

December, January, February: blue, purple, or evergreen

March, April, May: sea foam green, yellow, violet

June, July, August: lapis (it's a blue), ruby, aquamarine

September, October, November: barn red, goldenrod, aubergine

Of course, if you have a favorite color, you can use that. I hope it's in the correct season.

The secondary color should be a softer color such as cream, ivory, tan, or a paler version of your main color. The one exception would be black. Black could be your main color if your wedding is an evening event. You can go bold and use a metallic for your secondary color, which will be very good around the winter holidays. For example, lime green and copper is exquisite, but only use if lime green works with your coloring, which brings me to part two of color consideration.

Compliment to bride:

Coordinate the color scheme with YOU, not your attendants. If your redheaded sister-in-law-to-be will look bad in amber, so be it. This day is for you, and the worse she looks, the better you appear. Why do you think, traditionally, bridesmaids' dresses are so ugly?

DRESSING

You could choose your bridesmaids' dresses to be your secondary color with a waistband of the main color which would be quite extraordinary. This works better in the warmer seasons.

Whereas guys just get off "free" by only renting a tux or suit, women generally buy a dress (a dress so horrible, it will never be seen again). The style will depend on the formality of your wedding and the time of day. An evening wedding will be more formalwear and a lower hemline. I am not a fan of mix-matched bridesmaid's dress styles or colors. How is single Cousin Terrance to know who is in your wedding party or not? How will he be able to mingle with your attendants without being able to start a conversation with, "How do you know my cousin the bride?"

YOUR DRESS

I cannot say how you should dress, and the styles are SO numerous, I am not even going to address this. Besides, you will know your dress once it is on. Done & done.

GROOM & GROOMSMEN

The groomsmen's ties should match YOUR main color. The groom's tie should be the secondary color, except black, and then default to white. A groom in a white suit isn't fooling anyone. Even if he IS a virgin at the time of the wedding, his thoughts have surely tarnished him. Trust me.

MOTHER OF THE BRIDE

She can wear whatever she wishes, as long as it's not white (or your dress color) and follows the style of the wedding. No tea length for evening wedding.

MOTHER OF THE GROOM

Beige.

FLORALS

Flowers can provide freshness, a bit of nature, elegance, and sophistication. You can spend a lot of money on them, too. You could find a wholesaler, flower mart, or a farmers' market and assemble your own arrangements. You'll want to coordinate with your color scheme. Be mindful, the flowers and greenery have meanings. For example, if you're of Scottish decent, you may want to include globe thistle or use rosemary sprigs in your bouquet, the symbol of remembrance, as a tribute to your late grandmother. The very popular rose is generally a symbol of love, but color will vary the meaning: red - true love, white - purity or innocence, pink - grace, and yellow - friendship... I suspect your groom is more than a friend. If your color is yellow, might I suggest using yellow tulips symbolizing hopeless love? It's a far better option than just friendship. If your color is orange, I'd avoid marigolds, the symbol of pain and grief. Avoid daffodils or narcissus, which symbolize uncertainty or selfishness.

Two of the most striking flowers are the Casablanca lily, a large all white lily, and its relative the Stargazer, a pink and white lily. Both are extremely fragrant; so fragrant, many a bride will swoon due to its potent perfume. Keep this in mind when choosing your flowers, too, not only for your bouquet, but also the groomsmen's boutonnieres. A columbine is the symbol of faithlessness or ingratitude. Let's not use that for him.

Your bouquet ought to be larger than your bridesmaids' – again, this is your day. To save funds, you could supply them with a single long stemmed flower, or a small grouping of three stemmed flowers wrapped in coordinating ribbon. Simple is elegant. We don't live in Victorian England, do we? Just don't overdue the trailing ribbon. We don't want the cradled bouquets to appear as if the ladies are carrying micro-May Day poles.

Centerpieces will use a large portion of your floral budget. Simple bubble bowls with a floating flower will be elegant and cost effective, not to be confused with "cheap." If you're like so many newlyweds nowadays and moving into a new home, why not use potted plants that you'll use to landscape your new home? Waste not, want not. I'll discuss more on centerpieces later.

THEME WEDDINGS

Don't! It's goofy and temporary, like a fad. You'll reminisce and wonder, "Why did we do a Harry Potter themed wedding?" The one exception of theme-ing your wedding, would be style-wise. Just don't expect your guests to dress in kind. If you're getting married at a renaissance festival, have the wedding party dress in garb, but don't expect Grandpa Norman to don a codpiece. He won't do it, and no one wants to see that. A 1940's theme would be a great homage to your grandparents – especially if you're in her gown.

RECEPTION

Here is where my catering experience in a rental venue will provide my discerning suggestions. Choosing a venue for the reception depends on options in your area and time. Some venues could be booked years in advance, the same as large cathedrals. If the site is different than the ceremony, it would be good to have it easily attainable from the wedding. It will depend how soon after the ceremony. A morning wedding will leave a lot of time before a dinner. You could have your photographs taken during this time, while family and friends get lunch. Quite often people do an afternoon wedding so guests don't have to leave children dressed in their best all day. Just be sure YOU get some lunch. This is twofold – food for sustenance and alcohol absorption; a drunk bride is never pretty. I would even suggest a lot of starches – a mashed potato bar or thick breads and cheeses. You will not eat much before your ceremony, but you will have champagne afterwards. Insist your groom and his party starch up, too. A blithering drunk toast is never remembered, just the drunk. As your guests await your arrival, provide some hors d'oeuvres or suggest in the invitation to nosh before your arrival at the venue. Excellent offerings would be mini pizzas, spinach dip and sourdough, or bruschetta. Notice how they contain bread? You'll want a bar available, but have it a cash bar to prevent lush Cousin Ashley from drinking it all. Perhaps provide a two drink ticket after the meal, if you feel hospitable. You can save money by just offering beer, wine, and a signature cocktail. You won't need to supply a full bar, a huge cost savings. Of course, wine could be offered at dinner. Keg beer is only fun in a frat house. As a cater waiter, I don't enjoy toweling up after sloppy sloshing drunks who tend to dance on me while I'm attempting to clean up their spills on the dance floor. Don't get me started on breakage of glassware while females insist on dancing without their shoes. Give them flats! If anything, *you* should be in flats. In a long gown, who's going to see those heels anyhow! Why do drunks insist on holding drinks AND dancing?

MEAL SERVICE

Buffets are a little cheaper overall, since you won't need as many staff, but food costs are higher since there is no portion control. Let's be honest, it seems cheap. Your guests feel like cattle, children get antsy waiting for the table's release, and heaven forbid, if the last table doesn't get the main item because big Cousin Bertha took too many meat items. Served meals are more memorable and feel more formal. I believe it is worth the extra price. Your guests can have a choice. JUST be sure to inquire about special dietary needs. A new trend is to have a heavy hors d'oeurves meal, either buffet or butler passed. This will be very Downton Abbey-esque. This would be great for mingling and socializing, but not if you have a lot of children.

For meal service, remember, as the bride, you are THE first to be served in all courses. We had an event where the young bride had a substantial lunch and refused the salad. Her wait person had to explain unless the salad was set down; no one else would be served.

Keep in mind timelines and service. I was working a table with only the wedding couple. At the time to serve the entrée, the bride decided to go use the restroom. So my co-server and I had to stand there with the wedding couple's covered meals, eyeing our fellow wait staff to cease and desist any service. So pee after the salad is served. Your salad won't get cold. When your plate is removed, another will be coming very shortly.

SPECIAL MEALS

You don't want a guest to starve because of your menu of milk/dairy, nut-encrusted, and gluten-filled food. You think they'll tell you, but they won't. They'll just ask a week before you've finalized your meals with your sales person and everything has been ordered. People think a rental hall is a restaurant, and cooks are standing by anticipating strange requests. If one of your guests forgets sautéed salmon with fresh herb pesto is made with pine nuts, the chefs will know; but if he isn't told of the nut allergy, how is he to prepare? I have often rushed back to the kitchen to ask if the plate contained such-and-such an item. The chefs will let us know if it's safe to serve, but that does slow down service. You know, we servers discuss this amongst ourselves afterwards: "I had this guest ask me 'Do the mashed potatoes contain dairy?' with a pat of butter on the top!" Or, "One of my guests asked 'Is the breaded chicken gluten free'?"

Be sure to check with your sales person to ensure you're able to list the most frequent allergens in your invitation. If you have a vegetarian who can't eat gluten... the grilled vegetables on couscous won't work, as couscous is baked pasta... pasta made from wheat... wheat contains gluten.

Here is a sample of an actual extra-ordinary menu:

Guest count: 84

Salad: **Mixed green salad** with fresh berries, parmesan and balsamic vinaigrette (74)
Dairy free salad (no parmesan – 7)
Yeast free salad (no parmesan, olive oil on side – 3)

Entrée: **Bone in roasted chicken** with cippolini onion, baby red potatoes, and mild miso-mustard sauce (10)
Braised beef short ribs, faro, root vegetable, brussel leaves, almonds, roasted garlic au jus (22)
Sautéed salmon with fresh herb pesto, Yukon gold potatoes, crème fraiche and asparagus (25)

Special entrées: **Plain grilled chicken breast** with green beans and baked potato (18)
Braised beef short ribs, faro, root vegetable with no almonds (2)
Salmon -- no dairy – with pesto, Yukon gold potatoes, and asparagus (1)
Salmon – no pesto –with green beans and baby red potatoes (1)
Grilled vegetables on saffron couscous drizzled with charmoula oil (4)
Grilled vegetables on saffron couscous drizzled with charmoula oil, NO ONION (1)

STAGING THE RECEPTION:

Your guests will head to the reception, but for the benefit of time and fluidity, do have the tables labeled and numbered easily seen from across the room. One wedding I worked did years (1995, 1996, etc.) with their portraits. Very cute, but where do you begin? They had the years all scrambled in no discernible order. We had guests asking us where "1987" was. If that wasn't confusing enough, they printed the years in different fonts. If you're going to stray from table numbers, make sure your guests can see them from a distance. Another wedding did movie titles by placing mini movie poster in holders on tables. I assume they were movie buffs, but we had so many guests wandering around trying to find Mall Rats or Pulp Fiction (by the way, they were next to each other). If guests asked the wait staff where The Exorcist was, we would respond with, "I believe the couple intended on you mingling with each other while looking for your table," mostly because we only knew the five tables we were assigned. Another thing about that event, the movies were all weird: The Exorcist, Kiss Kiss Bang Bang, Terminator 2 (not the original by the way). I would expect more love-themed cinematic titled movies for a wedding. If you insist on straying from the standard, place them in alphabetical order.

CENTERPIECES

Centerpieces should be (as you can assume) in the middle of the table but should not be too tall as to block the sightline of your guests with their table mates. There is not steadfast rule that dictates you must use flowers. One wedding I worked used little tiered cakes with the table numbers. Then the bride randomly assigned a guest at each table to cut and serve cake for the table. This is great for us, and saves you the cost of a staff member solely assigned to cutting cake and time serving dessert.

Assuming a sit down service, be mindful that aside from the centerpiece, you'll have settings (flatware, glassware, napkins, bread & butter plates, coffee cup and saucer), salt and pepper shakers, bread basket, butter dish, creamer and sugar, plus votive candles and the aforementioned table number. You may be adding party favors and possibly a menu card. With all this on the table, is there even room for the meal?

NAMECARDS/MEAL IDENTIFIERS

If you have a plated meal, you'll have to provide place cards with the guests' names and some identifier indicating what their meal choice is. Let's be clear... make your symbols clear! Seriously, I had a wedding where the menu choices were indicated with matching daisy stickers with colors varying for meal options: white, ivory, ecru, buff, tan, and grey. Once we dimmed the lighting for ambience and with flickering candles, they really looked the same (except for the grey, of course, but that option was a kid's menu... and a little person is a pretty good indicator).

Another example is when the party used gems. A clear gem was a symbol for the chicken dish, a black for beef, and purple for the vegetarian option. Again, in the dim lighting how could we tell the black and purple apart? Oh yes, the bridal colors were black and teal. Don't they make teal gems?

Similarly, we had a wedding whose meal indicators were black, navy, dark green, and purple. Again, remember the lighting will be dimmed. If you insist on going with colors in the same hue of the color wheel, why not vary the symbols or shapes. You could use daisies, lilies, and tulips for spring weddings, or leaf shapes in autumn. If you enjoy wine, use wine bottle shapes, cork screws, and wine glasses.

When a party had open seating and marked their meal option with the initial of their main course, I was approached by a women asking where table "C" was. I had to reply, with a straight face, "That is your entrée ma'am. You are having chicken."

One time we had a wedding that used scrollwork. The scrolling decoration to the right of the name card would symbolize chicken, the left side - pork tenderloin, and above - the vegetarian option. Kid's meals were without decoration. So the wait staff had to come up with mnemonics (a memory trick) to remember which meant what:

"It's *right* to have chicken, vegetarians are over the *top*, and you're *left* with pork. Kids are good for *nothing*."

It's just a trick to remember symbols. We don't really believe children are good for nothing -- unless they're all running around while we're carrying ten meals on oval trays, maneuvering in a serpentine path between chairs of opposing tables.

Here is a true example of a wedding that used stickers:

> **Free range chicken** with taleggio parsley sauce, Yukon gold smashers, and green beans with toasted almonds – Dove (Alright... that is ok to understand. A dove's a bird. A chicken is a bird.)

> **Saffron pappardelle pasta** with roasted tomatoes, artichoke and mushroom – Heart (Um... a vegetarian meal is more "healthy" for your heart...and artichokes have hearts. A little stretch, but I can make a connection.)

> **Pan seared pork tenderloin** with hard apple cider sauce, rosemary potato galette and fire roasted vegetables – Bell (Hmmm... a bell? Not sure how to make a connection.)

> **Peanut butter and jelly wraps** with chips -- gingerbread man – kid's meal (Kids like cookies...ok.)

> **Grilled cheese sandwich** with chips -- Turtle (Really? A *second* kid's meal? And a turtle??)

These sticker options would work if it was around Christmas time (bell/gingerbread men/dove) but the turtle tosses that idea out, AND it was in mid-July!

Here is basic and simple color code for food options:
  Red = beef (red meat)
  Yellow = chicken (color of feed or baby chicks)
  Pink = pork (pigs are pink)
  Fish = blue (water is blue)
  Vegetarian = green (color of foliage)

A great help for us servers would be if you, your mother, or planner would provide your guests' names, meal options, and their table. This way we wouldn't need to dart around the tables, circling like buzzards trying to decipher what sticker, color, gem, scrollwork, or symbol coordinate with menu item. If there are bizarre dietary needs, we will have them all typed out and clear for the simplest of server.

DESSERT

This is a no brainer – cake. I've already talked about how you can combine the centerpiece and table number and save on service cost and time. The days of huge towering tiered cakes are in the past. Most will do a smaller cake for the ceremonial cutting and offer slices of much cheaper sheet cakes. I do hope the fad of cupcakes is past us, but a recent trend of offering two flavors, one vanilla-based and one chocolate-based cake is a disturbance. Why you ask? When we serve split flavors, we serve every other guest. Inevitably, someone who is served the vanilla cake wants chocolate or vice versa -- it's as if they think they're at a restaurant. We kindly set the cake down and direct them to coerce their flavor choice from their neighbor. We are too busy. We have to serve coffee to all the guests before the toasts start.

Toasts/Groom's Dinner

I remember when the best man was the only person who gave a speech. Then for sexual equality, the maid/matron of honor started. Then the parents joined in, thanking people for coming and celebrating. Then some of the wedding party were added. So why not include the wedding couple, too? Pretty soon the toasts will become open mike night at some beatnik coffee shop.

My complaint is that toasts happen right after dinner and before dessert....or during dessert. People don't eat at the same rate, so if half the room is eating dessert and the other half has meal plates still in front, it is distracting. It's extremely difficult to serve a second cup of coffee to Grandma when someone at her table is toasting. While we are trying to serve your guests, we have to step aside until all the speeches are over. Keep the number of toasts to a limit. The father of the bride, as the financial host, should be the only parent speaking by thanking the guests for coming. Bridal parties shouldn't give toasts because they mainly talk about inside stories about college. Your Great Aunt Blanche doesn't need to hear about your drunken escapades, the groom's college nick-name of "The Shred," and having him prove it by showing off his abs. You and your new spouse shouldn't be giving toasts. Your time is at the groom's dinner. That is when you thank your parties for standing up for you and, traditionally, sharing your gifts. This is where extended family can do family traditions, such as the couple drinking out of great grandparents champagne flutes. You can thank your guests in your (aptly named) thank you cards.

Post Matrimony

After your big day, you're not done yet. You have all that loot to open and enjoy. You know you're judging how much your friends and relatives love you based on the haul. Most often, couples will have immediate family present for a brunch during this event, but keeping track of who gave what can be a Herculean task. So have your maid (matron) of honor and/or best man (if not too hung over) record what you received and from whom.

This way you can imbibe all the thrills of opening each item (and maybe a mimosa or two) and not be snarled in a briar of unwrapping, reading card, showing off the presents to those in attendance, and writing down each item and the sender. Might I suggest you do this opening party in your home? This way you won't have to handle the gifts, yet another time. Once the extended family has departed, you can refer to the notes and respond with confidence and tranquility. A great ending to your most important party on your most important day, filled with elegance and free of stress. Begin your new adventure of married life.

www.ingramcontent.com/pod-product-compliance
Lightning Source LLC
Chambersburg PA
CBHW060550030426
42337CB00021B/4514